The Bridge of Fire by James Elroy Flecker

James Elroy Flecker was born on 5th November 1884, in Lewisham, London.

Flecker does not seem to have enjoyed academic study and achieved only a Third-Class Honours in Greats in 1906. This did not set him up for a job in either government service or the academic world.

After some frustrating forays at school teaching he attempted to join the Levant Consular Service and entered Cambridge to study for two years. After a poor first year he pushed forward in the second and achieved First-Class honours. His reward was a posting to Constantinople at the British consulate.

However, Flecker's poetry career was making better progress and he was beginning to garner praise for his poems including The Bridge of Fire. Unfortunately, he was also showing the first symptoms of contracting tuberculosis. Bouts of ill health were to now alternate with periods of physical well-being woven with mental euphoria and creativity.

Before his early death he managed to complete several volumes of poetry, which he continually revised, together with some prose works and plays. It was a small canon of work but on his death on 3rd January 1915, of tuberculosis, in Davos, Switzerland he was described as "unquestionably the greatest premature loss that English literature has suffered since the death of Keats".

Index of Contents

TO JACK BEAZLEY

Poetae tenero, meo sodali

Gentle Poet, only friend,
Lover of the stars and sun,
Since our days are at an end,
Since the older days are done;

Since it seems that nevermore
May I hope to trail my gown
Rapturously, as before,
With my friend in Oxford Town;

Since I so regret a time
So unprofitably spent,
Let me send a little rhyme
From a king in banishment,

Send a wish that we may see
Better days, and braver days:
Florcas, amice mil
Floreat Praxitelts.

I

A New Year's Carol

Awake, awake! The world is young,

For all its weary years of thought:
The starkest fights must still be fought,
The most surprising songs be sung.

And those who have no other Gods
May still behold, if they bestir,
The windy amphitheatre
Where dawn the timeless periods.

Then hear the shouting- voice of men
Magniloquently rise and ring:
Their flashing eyes and measured swing
Prove that the world is young again.

I was beyond the hills, and heard
That old and fervent Goddess call,
Whose voice is like a waterfall,
And sweeter than the singing-bird.

O stubborn arms of rosy youth,
Break down your other Gods, and turn
To where her dauntless eyeballs burn, —
The silent pools of Light and Truth.

II

Rioupéroux

High and solemn mountains guard Riouperoux,
Small untidy village where the river drives a mill:
Frail as wood-anemones, white and frail were you,
And drooping a little like the slender daffodil.

Oh I will go to France again, and tramp the valley through,
And I will change these gentle clothes for clog and corduroy,
And work with the mill-hands of black Riouperoux,
And walk with you and talk with you like any other boy.

III

The Ballad of the Student in the South

It was no sooner than this morn
That first I found you there,

Up to your breast in Southern corn
As golden as your hair.

I had read books you had not read,
Yet was I put to shame
To hear the simple words you said,
That shuddered like a flame.

Shall I forget, when prying dawn
Sends me about my way,
The careless stars, the quiet lawn,
And you with whom I lay?

Darling, a Scholar's fancies sink
All faint beneath your song:
And you are right: why should we think,
We who are young and strong?

We're of the people, you and I,
We do what others do,
Linger and toil, and laugh and die,
And love the whole night through.

IV

Mignon

Knowst thou the land where bloom the Lemon-trees,
And darkly gleam the golden oranges?
A gentle wind blows down from that blue sky;
Calm stands the Myrtle and the Laurel high.
Hast thou been there? Away, away!
O Father, let us seek that land some day.

Knowst thou the House, that gloriously glows
With shining rooms and pillared porticoes.
The marble statues stand and look at me:
Alas, poor child, what hath been done to thee?
Hast thou been there? Away, away!
Together let us go, brave friend, some day!

Knowst thou the Mountain with its crown of cloud?
The mule plods warily; the white mists shroud;
Coiled in their caves the ancient Dragons dream:
Down leaps the rock, and over it the stream.
Hast thou been there? Away, away!

There lies our path. O Father, come to-day!

(From Goethe)

V

Dorothy

Dorothy, open your sweet eyes,
Give me your mouth to kiss:
Tell me how women get so wise,
And what their secret is.

Yours is the beauty of the moon,
The wisdom of the sea,
Since first you tasted, sweet and soon,
Of God's forbidden tree.

VI

From Grenoble

Now have I seen, in Graisivaudan's vale,
The fruits that dangle and the vines that trail,
The poplars standing up in bright blue air,
The silver turmoil of the broad I sere
And sheer pale cliffs that wait through Earth's long noon
Till the round Sun be colder than the Moon.

Mine be the ancient song of Travellers:
I hate this glittering land where nothing stirs:
I would go back, for I would see again
Mountains less vast, a less abundant plain,
The Northern Cliffs clean-swept with driven foam,
And the rose-garden of my gracious home.

VII

Hialmar Speaks to the Raven

Night on the bloodstained snow: the wind is chill;
And there a thousand tombless warriors lie,

Grasping their swords, wild-featured: all are still:
Above them the black ravens wheel and cry.

A brilliant moon sends her cold light abroad:
Hialmar arises from the reddened slain,
Leaning heavily on his shattered sword,
And bleeding from his side the battle-rain.

"Hail to you all: is there one breath still drawn
Among those fierce and fearless lads that played
So merrily, and sang as sweet in the dawn
As thrushes singing in the bramble shade?

"They have no word to say: my helm's unbound,
My breastplate by the axe unriveted:
Blood's on my eyes; I hear a spreading sound
Like waves or wolves that clamour in my head.

"Eater of men, old raven, come this way,
And with thine iron bill open my breast:
To-morrow find us as we are to-day,
And bear my heart to her that I love best.

"Through Upsala, where drink the Jarls and sing,
And clash their golden bowls in company,
Bird of the moor, carry with tireless wing
To Ylmer's daughter there the heart of me.

"And thou shalt see her standing, straight and pale,
High-pedestalled on some rook-haunted tower:
She has two earrings wrought of silver scale,
And eyes like stars that shine in twilight hour.

"Tell her my love, thou dark bird ominous;
Give her my heart, no bloodless heart and vile,
But red, compact and strong, O raven. Thus
Shall Ylmer's daughter greet thee with a smile.

"Now let my life from twenty deep wounds flow,
And wolves may drink the blood. My time is done.
Young, brave and spotless, laughing-free I go
To sit where all the Gods are, in the sun."

"Le coeur de Hialmar" Leconte de Lisle.

We that were friends to-night have found
A sudden fear, a secret flame:
I am on fire with the soft sound
You make, in uttering my name.

Forgive a young and boastful man
Whom dreams delight and passions please,
And love me as great women can,
Who have no children at their knees.

IX

Pervigilium

Reign, thou marble Venus, reign!
We are tired of painted Marys.
Thou shalt stir thyself again,
And be queen of our vagaries.
Men no more shall worship pain
When they taste how brave the air is,
When they herald thee with laughter, and with roses entertain.

When thy lilies bloom once more,
When thy bosomed rosebuds waken,
Love shall be our only lore,
Cares and creeds be all forsaken;
And we'll wander by the shore,
Up among the forest bracken,
Decked with leaf and crowned with branches, children as we were before.

When the world returns to Spring,
In the commonwealth of races
Every Poet shall be King
With a court of happy faces:
Maidens in a rosy ring
Shall be lavish of embraces;
Every night shall throb with music: all the reeling world shall sing.

I must dream no more to-day:
Children, home! we cannot sever
Pain and Grief and Death whose sway
Stands unalterable ever.
Though you roam the woods alway,
Vain is love, and vain endeavour.
Sorrow breathes among the woodland; whispers break upon our play.

X

I have sung all Love's great songs,
And have no new song to sing,
But I'll sing the old songs again,
With their burden of rights and wrongs,
And conventional sad refrain,—
O, sweet Love's home-coming!

I will praise the arms of my Love,
And her tender body's swing,
And her eyes, and her lips and breath:
I will call to the powers above,
And to tunnelling powers beneath,—
O sweet Love's home-coming!

Thus did we, and always will,
While centuries crowd on the wing,
And drive us along to our doom,
When the globes shall be ground in the Mill
And lovers shall leap from the tomb, —
O, sweet Love's home-coming!

XI

On Turner's Polyphemus

Painter of day, let my dark spirit fly
Past the Trinacrian Sound, to gaze upon
The deathless horses of Hyperion
Driven up fiery stairs tumultuously:
To see once more the Achaian prows glide by,
Odysseus in his burnished galleon,
Nereides that sing him swiftly on,
And baffled Cyclops fading in the sky.

Master, you paint the passion of the Earth,
The faint victorious music of her birth,
The splendour of things lost and things grown old;
And show us song new-wrought with ardent might
Of strong-winged morning and of sure delight,
Of hyacinthine mist, and shining gold.

XII

To Francis Thompson

With a grey rush of tremulous angel-wings
And pealings of the white-robed orchestra
Wherein ethereal souls were playing a
Concerto of divine imaginings:
With freshness born anew from old-time Springs,
With Summer's flash and Winter's purity,
With Autumn's gentleness he came to me,
And whispered words of visionary things.
Till shafts of dim desire pierced me through,
Till shadows came and went before my eyes,
And my raised glance beheld in deep review
The legionary splendour of the skies.
Which vision past, singing I went my way
And tread the dusty roads of Earth to-day.

XIII

The Ballad of Hampstead Heath

From Heaven's gate to Hampstead Heath
Young Bacchus and his crew
Came tumbling down, and o'er the town
Their bursting trumpets blew.

The silver night was wildly bright,
And madly shone the moon,
To hear a song so clear and strong,
With such a lovely tune.

From London's houses, huts, and flats
Came busmen, snobs, and Earls,
And ugly men in bowler hats
With charming little girls.

Sir Moses came, with eyes of flame,
Judd, who is like a bloater,
The brave Lord Mayor, in coach and pair,
King Edward, in his motor.

Far in a rosy mist withdrawn

The God, and all his crew,
Silenus pulled by nymphs, a faun,
A satyr drenched in dew,

Smiled as they wept those shining tears
Only Immortals know,
Whose feet are set among the stars,
Above the shifting snow.

And one spake out into the night
Before they left for ever,
"Rejoice, rejoice!" and his great voice
Rolled like a splendid river.

He spoke in Greek, which Britons speak
Seldom, and circumspectly;
But Mr. Judd, that man of mud,
Translated it correctly.

And when they heard that happy word
Policemen leapt and ambled:
The busmen pranced, the maidens danced,
The men in bowlers gambolled.

An Echo walked the town till late,
And found the long streets lonely:
At last she found a small brass plate
Inscribed FOR MEMBERS ONLY.

And so she went to Parliament;
But those ungainly men
Woke up from sleep, and turned about,
And fell asleep again.

XIV

Ideal

When all my gentle friends had gone
I wandered in the night alone:
Beneath the green electric glare
I saw men pass with hearts of stone;
Yet still I heard them everywhere,
The golden voices of the air:
"Friend, we will go to hell with thee,
Thy griefs, thy glories we will share,

And rule the land and shake the sea
And set a thousand devils free:"
"What dost thou, Stranger, at my side,
Thou gaunt old man accosting me?
Away, this is my night of pride!
On Satan's horses I will ride,
And I will seek delightful things."
The old man answered: "Woe betide!
Said I, "The world is made for Kings:
To him who works and working sings
Come joy and majesty and power
And steadfast love with royal wings."
"O watch these fools that blink and cower,"
Said that wise man:" and every hour
A score is born, a dozen dies."
Said I: "In London fades the flower
But far away the bright blue skies
Shall watch my solemn walls arise,
And all the glory, all the grace
Of earth shall gather there, and eyes
Will shine like stars in that new place."
Said he: "Indeed of ancient race
Thou comest, with thy hollow scheme:
And quiet tears of men shall stream
For thee, O Architect of Dream,
Where are the islands of the blest?
And where Atlantis, where Theleme?"

XV

Arthur Rackham's Rip Van Winkle

Since youth is wise, and cannot comprehend
Proportion, nor behold things as they are,
Φιλοθεάμονες we'll be, my friend,
And laugh at what appears quadrangular,
Our only Gods shall be the Subterrane,
Pictures of things misshapen, harsh and crude,
The flattened Face outside the window-pane,
The little Squeak behind us in the wood.
Here, friend, are subtly drawn uncommon things:
Make such your Gods: they only understand.
Only a Headless Wag with slimy wings
Can stop your toothache and the Dentist's hand.
Though after twenty years they may not please,
Sane men have worshipped stranger Gods than these.

XVI

Mary Magdalen

O eyes that strip the souls of men!
There came to me the Magdalen.
Her blue robe with a cord was bound,
Her hair with Lenten lilies crowned.
"Arise," she said, "God calls for thee:
Turned to new paths thy feet must be.
Leave the fever and the feast,
Leave the friends thou lovest best.
For thou must walk in barefoot ways
To give my dear Lord Jesus praise."

Then answered I "Sweet Magdalen,
God's servant, once beloved of men,
Why didst thou change old ways for new,
Thy trailing red for corded blue,
Roses for lilies on thy brow,
Rich splendour for a barren vow?"

Gentle of speech she answered me:
"Sir, I was sick with revelry.
True, I have scarred the night with sin,
A pale and tawdry heroine;
But once I heard a voice that said
"Who lives in sin is surely dead,
But whoso turns to follow Me
Hath joy and immortality.' "

"O Mary, not for this," I cried,
"Didst thou renounce thy scented pride.
Not for a prize of endless years,
Or barren joy apart from tears
Didst thou desert the courts of men.
Tell me thy truth, sweet Magdalen!"
She trembled, and her eyes grew dim:
"For love of Him, for love of Him."

XVII

I rose from dreamless hours and sought the morn

That beat upon my window: from the sill
I watched sweet lands where Autumn light new-born
Swayed through the trees and lingered on the hill.

If things so lovely are, why labour still
To dream of something more than this I see?
Do I remember tales of Galilee,
I who have slain my faith and freed my will?

Let me forget dead faith, dead mystery,
Dead thoughts of things I cannot comprehend.
Enough the light mysterious in the tree,
Enough the faithful friendship of my friend.

XVIII

The Bridge of Fire

I

Past the bright door of Heaven whose golden bars
Exclude the interchange of Night and Day,
Crowned with soft light, attired with shining stars,
Dwell the great Gods in durable array.
In all that land no frost, no fever mars
Their timeless periods of pomp and play:
Some drive about the Rim in painted cars,
And others drink eternity away.
      The trumpet of their pride
      Proclaims them glorified
In chronicles of unremembered sway;
      And lady Goddesses
      Surround with sweet caress
Their ivied paramours. "O rest!" they say:

"Here at our gentle bosoms lie,
And watch the sun and moon and world and years roll by!"

II

Hear now the song of those bright shapes that shine
Huge as Leviathans, tasting the fare
Delicate-sweet, while scented dews divine
Thrill from the ground and clasp the rosy air.
"Sing on, sing out, and reach a hand for wine!

For the drunken Earth spins softly afloat down there,
And the stars burn low, and the sky is sapphirine,
And the little winds of Space are in our hair!
        The little winds of Space
        Blow in the Love-god's face,
The only God that lacks not praise and prayer;
        Who sole preserves his power
        While dynasties devour
Temples and shrines and stones without repair.
Still he goes forth as strong as ten,
A red immortal riding in the hearts of men!"

III

The Gods whose names are sunrise and delight
For him who loves the leafy ways of song,
The Gods of Hellas have escaped the night
To walk above the stars, a royal throng,
Zeus and Poseidon and the Boy most bright,
The twain to whom the sceptred shades belong,
Majestical Princesses famed in fight,
And Aphrodite sweet to charm the strong:
        And younger Gods than these
        That peep among the trees,
And dance when Dionysus beats his gong:
        And old disastrous Gods
        That nod with snaky nods,
Allecto swift to strike with dripping throng:
Itself the dull profound of Hell
Spits reeling Typhon forth that in the dark did dwell.

IV

Shadows there are that seem to look for home,
Each one a gloom upon the stellar plain,
Voiced like a great bell swinging in a dome,
Appealing mightily for realms to reign.
One said "These are the shapeless Gods of Rome,
The tired-out Gods of labour, sweat and pain:
These watched the peasant turn his sullen loam,
These dragged him forth to fight and strive again,
        Saturnus white and old,
        Who lost the age of gold,
Mars and Minerva standing on the slain,
        Pomona from whose womb

The fruits in season come,
And she who gathers in the mellow grain,
And ghouls of the revengeful dead,
Larvae and Lemures that clamour to be fed."

V

Belus and Ra and that most jealous Lord
Who rolled the hosts of Pharaoh in the sea,
Giants and Trolls, in every hand a sword,
Gnomes and Dwarfs and the Spectral Company,
Gods that take vengeance, Gods that grant reward,
Gods that exact a murdered devotee,
Buddha the Wise, and Siva the Abhorred,
And Norns that tend Ygdrasil, fatal tree,
    And Isis of the Moon
    Who kept the stars in tune,
With her mad Phrygian sister, Cybele,
    And Mithras swift to save
    The faithful and the brave,
And Allah rumbling on to victory,
Behold! and oldest of them all,
Square heads that leer and lust, and lizard shapes that crawl.

VI

The astral light grows dim upon the dales,
As he who loved the sinner and the child,
Before whose beauty still the tyrant quails
Comes by alone, a quiet man and mild.
The voice of all reproach is fixed and fails;
The heart is willing to be reconciled.
Was it his work, the groaning in the jails?
When bodies writhed and wept, could he have smiled?
    Be strong, undaunted soul,
    To break the aureole:
Release our chain, but leave him unreviled.
    Though sweet the lily blows
    The fire upon the rose
Alone shall guide thee on the bitter wild,
At last to find no Lotus land,
But one where Truth may touch thee dying with sweet hand.

VII

Between the pedestals of Night and Morning,
Between red Death and radiant Desire,
With clamour of delight and doubt and warning
The High Gods stand upon the Bridge of Fire.
O Soul, lay down thy pride, and cease adorning
Thy brows with laurel or with gold thy lyre!
The wheels of Time are turning, turning, turning ;
The slow Stream waits for thee, the stagnant Mire.
   The Dreamer and his Dream
   Shall struggle in the Stream
Sunless and unredeemable for ever,
   Since this the Gods command,
   That he who leaves their land
Shall travel down to that relentless River.
"O Master of the World," I cry,
"Save me from fear of Death : I dare not die."

XIX

Narcissus

Thou with whom I dallied
Through all the hours of noon, —
Sweet water-boy, more pallid
Than any watery moon;
Above thy body turning
White lily-buds were strewn:
Alas, the silver morning,
Alas, the golden noon!
Alas, the clouds of sorrow,
The waters of despair!
I sought thee on the morrow,
And never found thee there.
Since first I saw thee splendid,
Since last I called thee fair,
My happy ways have ended
By waters of despair.
The pool that was thy dwelling
I hardly knew again,
So black it was, and swelling
With bitter wind and rain.
Amid the reeds I lingered
Between desire and pain
Till evening, rosy-fingered,
Beckoned to night again.

Yet once when sudden quiet
Had visited the skies,
And stilled the stormy riot,
I looked upon thine eyes.
I saw they wept and trembled
With glittering mysteries,
But yellow clouds assembled
Redarkening the skies.

O listless thou art lying
In waters cool and sweet,
While I, dumb brother, dying,
Faint in the desert heat.
Though thou dost love another,
Still let my lips entreat:
Men call me fair, O brother,
And women honey-sweet.

XX

The Golden Head

Had I the power
To Midas given of old
To touch a flower,
And leave the petals gold,
I then might touch thy face,
Delightful Maid,
And leave a metal grace,
A graven head.

Thus would I slay—
Ah, desperate device!
The vital day
That trembles in thine eyes,
And let the red lips close
That sang so well,
And drive away the rose,
To leave a shell.

Then I myself,
Rising austere and dumb,
On the high shelf
Of my half-lighted room
Would place the shining bust,
And wait alone,

Until I was but dust,
Buried unknown.

Thus, in my love
For nations yet unborn,
I would remove
From our two lives the morn,
And muse on old speeches
In mine armchair,
Content, should Time confess
How sweet you were.

XXI

Litany to Satan

(From Baudelaire)

O grandest of the Angels, and most wise,
O fallen God, fate- driven from the skies,
Satan, at last take pity on our pain!

O first of exiles who endurest wrong,
Who growest in thy hatred still more strong
Satan, at last take pity on our pain!

O subterranean King, omniscient,
Healer of Man's immortal discontent!
Satan, at last take pity on our pain!

To lepers and to outcasts thou dost show
How passion makes Man's Paradise below.
Satan, at last take pity on our pain!

Thou by thy Mistress Death hast given to man
Hope, the imperishable courtesan.
Satan, at last take pity on our pain!

Thou givest to the Guilty their calm mien
That damns the crowd around the guillotine.
Satan, at last take pity on our pain!

Thou knowest those corners of the jealous Earth
Where God has hidden jewels of great worth.
Satan, at last take pity on our pain!

Thou dost discover by mysterious signs
Where sleep the buried people of the mines.
Satan, at last take pity on our pain!

Thou stretchest forth a saving hand to keep
Such men as roam upon the roofs in sleep.
Satan, at last take pity on our pain!

Thy power can make the halting Drunkards' feet
Avoid the peril of the surging street.
Satan, at last take pity on our pain!

Thou to console our helplessness, didst plot
The cunning use of powder and of shot.
Satan, at last take pity on our pain!

Thy awful name is written as with pitch
On the unrelenting foreheads of the rich:
Satan, at last take pity on our pain!

In strange and hidden places thou dost move
Where passions welter in unhallowed love.
Satan, at last take pity on our pain!

Father of those whom God's tempestuous ire
Has flung from Paradise with sword and fire,
Satan, at last take pity on our pain!

PRAYER

Satan, to thee be praise upon the height
Where thou wast King of old, and in the night
Of Hell, where thou dost dream on silently.
Grant that one day beneath the knowledge tree,
When it bursts forth to grace thy royal brow,
My soul may sit, that cries upon thee now.

XXII

While I translated Baudelaire
Children were playing out in the air.
Turning to watch, I saw the light
That made their clothes and faces bright.
I heard the tune they tried to sing,
As they kept dancing in a ring;
But I could not forget my book,

And thought of men whose faces shook
When babies passed them with a look.

They are as terrible as death,
Those children in the road beneath.
Their witless chatter is more dread
Than voices in a madman's head:
Their dance more awful and inspired,
Because they are not ever tired,
Than silent revel with soft sound
Of pipes, on consecrated ground,
When all the ghosts go round and round.

XXIII

Prayer

Let me not know how sins and sorrows glide
Along the sober city of our rage,
Or why the sons of men are heavy-eyed.

Let me not know, except from printed page,
The pain of bitter Love, of baffled Pride,
Or Sickness shadowing with a long presage.

Let me not know, since happy some have died
Quickly in youth or quietly in age
How faint, how loud, the bravest hearts have cried.

XXIV

Tenebris Interlucentem

Once a poor songbird that had lost her way
Sang down in Hell upon a blackened bough,
Till all the lazy ghosts remembered how
The forest trees stood up against the day.

Then suddenly they knew that they had died,
Hearing this music mock their shadow land:
And some one there stole forth a timid hand
To draw a phantom brother to his side.

XXV

Anapaests

Songs rolling a harmony deeper
Than waves on a boreal shore,
Than reboant winds upon seas,
Battle-harmonies, rousing the sleeper
To war, from the dreaming of war,
I weary of songs such as these.

Physicians that need not a physic,
Star- voices atune with the morn,
The poet upstanding and strong,
Make drunk with celestial music,
Drive mad with their musical scorn,
The men who go bitterly wrong.

I hate the bright streams of perfection,
The words that are golden and wise,
Triumphantly noble in pain;
The Spirits in fierce insurrection,
But calm as the tent of the skies,
I hate, for I cannot attain.

Songs breathed to the tremulous ditties
Of broken and harsh violins,
Songs hinting the rose and the vine,
Half drowned in the roar of red cities,
And youthfully pleased at their sins,
These songs I adore : they are mine.

XXVI

Destroyer of Ships, Men, Cities

To I. D.

Helen of Troy has sprung from Hell
To claim her ancient throne:
So we have bidden friends farewell
To follow her alone.

The Lady of the laurelled brow,
The Queen of pride and power,

Looks rather like a spirit now,
And rather like a flower.

Dark in her eyes the lamp of night
Burns with a secret flame,
Where shadows pass that have no sight,
And ghosts that have no name.

For mute is battle's brazen horn
That rang for Priest and King;
And she who drank of that brave morn
Is pale with evening.

An hour there is when bright words flow,
A little hour for sleep,
An hour between, when lights are low,
And then she seems to weep.

But no less lovely than of old
She shines, and almost hears
The horns that blew in days of gold,
The shouting charioteers.

And still she breaks the hearts of men,
Their hearts, and all their pride,
Doomed to be cruel once again,
And live dissatisfied.

XXVII

My Friend

I had a friend who battled for the Truth,
With stubborn heart and obstinate despair,
Till all his beauty left him, and his youth,
And there were few that loved him anywhere.

Then would he wander out among the graves,
And dream of dead men lying in a row;
Or, standing on a cliff, observe the waves,
And hear the wistful sound of winds below;

And yet they told him nothing. So he sought
The twittering forest at the break of day,
Or on fantastic mountains shaped a thought
As lofty and impenitent as they.

And next he walked in wonder through the town,
Slowly by day and hurriedly by night,
To watch the puppets dangling up and down
With timorous and terrible delight.

Weary, he drew man's wisdom from a book,
And pondered on the high words spoken of old,
Pacing a lamplit room; but soon forsook
The golden sentences that left him cold.

After, a maiden found him, and his head
Lay on her breast, till he forgot his pain
In gentle kisses on a midnight bed,
And welcomed royal-winged Joy again.

When love became a loathing, as it must,
He knew not where to turn; and he was wise,
Being full of years, to mix himself with dust,
To rest his rebel soul, and close his eyes.

XXVIII

Oxford Canal

When you have wearied of the valiant spires of this County Town,
Of its wide white streets and glistening museums,
Of its red motors and lumbering trams and self-sufficient people,
I will take you walking with me to a place you have not yet seen
Half town and half country the lonely land of the Canal.
It is dearer to me than the antique town: I love it more than the rounded hills:
There is no river so straight or so unearthly as the long Canal.
No gloomy forest, no mysterious glen is so full of fear as that long line of sickly willows:
In forests and glens you may find unpleasant beasts and irregular demons,

But all through the autumn nights the souls of the lost pass through the willow-trees.
I have observed great storms and trembled: I have wept in the dark for fear,
But nothing makes me so afraid as the clear water of that empty Canal at noon.
Do you see the great telegraph poles down in the water how every wire is distinct?
If a body fell into the Canal it would rest entangled in those wires for ever, between earth and heaven:

For the water is as deep as the sky itself.
One day I was foolishly wondering how if a man fell off that lofty pole,
He would rush through the water towards me till the images were scattered by his splash,
When suddenly a train rushed by: the brazen dome of the engine flashed: the long white carriages roared ;

The sun veiled himself for a moment, and the signals loomed in fog;

A savage woman screamed at me from a barge: little children began to cry;
The untidy, unfinished land began to move: a saw-mill started;
A cart rattled down to the wharf, and workmen clanged over the iron foot-bridge;
A beautiful old man nodded from the first-story window of a square red house,
And a pretty girl came out to hang up clothes in a small delightful garden.
O strange motion in the suburb of a County Town: slow, regular movement of the dance of death!
No phantoms move in the light: more terrible than phantoms, they are men.
Theirs is no romance of great cities, or stupendous crimes ; nor do they live on wild poetic moors.
Forgotten they live, and forgotten die.

XXIX

The Old Poet

Now fails the fire: my heart is numb with pain:
I am reminded in too many ways
Of voices I shall never hear again,
Of happier days.

O not another poem will I write:
I will forget the books that I have read:
I will step out reluctant through the night,
Veiling my head.

For grief like mine no tragic peals of woe
Thunder: I am too cursed with abject fear
To stand in daylight. Of my poems know
This one sincere.

XXX

The Young Poet

If there be any grief
For those lost eremites
That live in lonely tombs,
It is on Autumn nights,
At falling of the leaf;
It is when pale October,
Relentless tree-disrober,
Invades the silent homes.

But him no Autumn's chill
Shall have the power to harm:
Predominant, his lyre
Shall keep remembrance warm
And leave him lovely still:
And spirits softly winging
Shall listen to his singing,
And weep for his desire.

He loved and sang and sinned
With roses on his brow.
Alas for all his pride!
His eyes are eaten now,
He's lighter than the wind.
The veil of Love is riven,
The Sin by Death forgiven,
The Singer glorified.

Autumn has killed the rose:
O mock him not with flowers:
Set up no shapely stone!
Take him to pass the hours
Where the grey nettle grows.
With scant and scarce adorning
Let him who praised the morning
Lie here, alone, unknown!

XXXI

The First Sonnet of Bathrolaire

Over the moonless land of Bathrolaire
Rises at night, when revelry begins,
A white unreal orb, a Sun that spins,
And watches with a faint metallic stare
The madly moving dance that they dance there,
Whilst din and drone of ghostly violins
Drown the triumphant shriek of obscene sins,
And raise the incantation of despair.

And all the spaces of that midnight Town
Sound with appeal and sorrowful abuse.
There some most lonely are: some try to crown
Mad lovers with sad boughs of formal yews,
And Titan women wandering up and down
Lead on the pale fanatics of the Muse,

XXXII

The Second Sonnet of Bathrolaire

Now the sweet Dawn on brighter fields afar
Has walked among the daisies, or has breathed
The glory of the mountain winds, and sheathed
The stubborn sword of Night's last-shining star.
In Bathrolaire, when Day's old doors unbar
The motley mask, fantastically wreathed
Pass through a strong portcullis, brazen-teethed,
And enter glowing mines of cinnabar.
Stupendous prisons shut them out from day,
Gratings and caves and rayless catacombs,
And the unrelenting rack and tourniquet
Grind death in cells where jetting gaslight gloams,
And iron ladders stretching far away
Dive to the depths of those eternal Domes.

XXXIII

I am afraid to think about my death,
When it shall be, and whether in great pain
I shall rise up and battle for my breath,
Or calmly wait the bursting of my brain.

I am no coward who should seek in fear
A folklore solace or sweet Indian tales :
I know dead men are deaf and cannot hear
The singing of a thousand nightingales.

I know dead men are blind, and cannot see
The friend that shuts in horror their big eyes,
And they are witless Oh, I'd rather be
A living mouse than dead in such a wise.

XXXIV

Envoy

The young men leap, and toss their golden hair,

Run round the land, or sail across the seas:
But one was stricken with a sore disease,
The lean and swarthy poet of despair.

Know me, the slave of fear and death and shame,
A sad Comedian, a most tragic Fool,
Shallow, imperfect, fashioned without rule,
The doubtful shadow of a demon flame.

AN ESSAY ON JAMES LEROY FLECKER by JC SQUIRE

In person Flecker was tall, with blue eyes, black, straight hair, and dark complexion. There was a tinge of the East in his appearance, and his habitual expression was a curious blend of the sardonic and the gentle. Until illness incapacitated him he was physically quite active, but his principal amusement was conversation, of which he never tired. He felt acutely the loss of good talk during his years abroad, in Syria especially. He was sociable, and enjoyed meeting and talking with crowds of people; but he had few intimate friends at Oxford, and, after he left England, little opportunity of making any. One of the few, Mr. Frank Savery, now of the British Legation, Berne, sends the following notes:

"My acquaintance with him began in January 1901, when he was a lanky, precocious boy of sixteen, and lasted, with long interruptions, until his death. His fate took him to the Near East, mine took me to Germany: for this reason we never met from 1908 to 1914, though we never ceased to correspond. Largely because our intercourse was thus broken, I believe that I am better able to appreciate the changes which his character underwent in the latter years of his life than those who never lost sight of him for more than a few months at a time.

"It was at Oxford that I first came to know him intimately. He was extraordinarily undeveloped, even for an English Public School boy, when he first went up in 1902. He already wrote verses—with an appalling facility that for several years made me doubt his talent. He imitated with enthusiasm and without discrimination, and, the taste in those long-gone days being for Oscar Wilde's early verse and Swinburne's complacent swing, he turned out a good deal of decadent stuff, that was, I am convinced, not much better than the rubbish written by the rest of his generation at Oxford. What interested me in Flecker in those days was the strange contrast between the man—or rather the boy—and his work. Cultured Oxford in general, I should add, was not very productive at that time: a sonnet a month was about the maximum output of the lights of Balliol. The general style of literature in favour at the time did not lend itself to a generous outpouring. Hence there was a certain piquancy in the exuberant flow of passionate verse which issued from Flecker's ever-ready pen in spite of his entire innocence of any experience whatever.

"Furthermore, he was a wit—a great wit, I used to think, but no humorist—and, like most wits, he was combative.

He talked best when some one baited him. At last it got to be quite the fashion in Oxford to ask Flecker to luncheon and dinner-parties—simply in order to talk. The sport he afforded was usually excellent.... Looking back on it now, I believe I was right in thinking that in those days he had no humour (there is very little humour in Oxford); nor am I so entirely sure that his wit was bad. I had, at any rate, a growing feeling that, in spite of his immaturity and occasional bad taste, he was the most important of any of us: his immense productiveness was, I vaguely but rightly felt, better and more valuable than our finicky and sterile good taste.

"By 1906 he had developed greatly—largely thanks to the companionship of an Oxford friend whom, in spite of long absence and occasional estrangements, he loved deeply till the end of his life. Even his decadent poems had improved: poor as are most of the poems in 'The Bridge of Fire,' they are almost all above the level of Oxford poetry, and there are occasional verses which forecast some of his mature work. Thus I still think that the title-poem itself is a rather remarkable achievement for a young man and not without a certain largeness of vision. The mention of this poem reminds me of an episode which well illustrates the light-heartedness which at that time distinguished the self-styled 'lean and swarthy poet of despair.' I was sitting with him and another friend in his rooms one day—early in 1906, I think—when he announced that he was going to publish a volume of poems. 'What shall I call it?' he asked. We had made many suggestions, mostly pointless, and almost all, I have no doubt, indecent, when Flecker suddenly exclaimed: 'I'll call it "The Bridge of Fire," and I'll write a poem with that name and put it in the middle of the book instead of the beginning. That'll be original and symbolic too.' We then debated the not unimportant question of what 'The Bridge of Fire' would be about. At midnight we parted, the question still unsettled. Flecker, however, remarked cheerfully that it did not much matter—it was a jolly good title and he'd easily be able to think of a poem to suit it.

"Flecker always cherished a great love for Oxford: he had loved it as an undergraduate, and afterwards not even the magic of the Greek seas, deeply as he felt it, ever made him forget his first university town. But on the whole I think that Cambridge, where he went to study Oriental languages in preparation for his consular career, did more for him. I only visited him once there—in November 1908, I think—but I had the distinct impression that he was more independent than he had been at Oxford. He was writing the first long version—that is to say, the third actual draft—of the 'King of Alsander.' Incidentally he had spoilt the tale, for the time being, by introducing a preposterous sentimental conclusion, a departure to unknown lands, if I remember rightly, with the peasant-maid, who had not yet been deposed, as she was later on, from her original position of heroine.

"And now follow the years in which my knowledge of Flecker is drawn only from a desultory correspondence. I should like to quote from some of the letters he wrote me, but, alas, they are in Munich with all my books and papers. He wrote to me at length whenever he had a big literary work on hand; otherwise an occasional post card sufficed, for he was a man who never put either news or gossip into his letters. I knew of his marriage; I knew that his literary judgment, as expressed in his letters and exemplified in his writings, had improved suddenly and phenomenally. That was all.

"At last his health finally collapsed and he came to Switzerland. It was at Locarno, in May 1914, that I saw him again. He was very ill, coughed continually, and did not, I think, ever go out during the whole fortnight I spent with him. He had matured even more than I had expected....

"He was very cheerful that spring at Locarno—cheerful, not extravagantly optimistic, as is the way of consumptives. I think he hardly ever mentioned his illness to me, and there was certainly at that time nothing querulous about him. His judgment was very sound, not only on bocks but also on men. He confessed that he had not greatly liked the East—always excepting, of course, Greece—and that his intercourse with Mohammedans had led him to find more good in Christianity than he had previously suspected. I gathered that he had liked his work as Consul, and he once said to me that he was very proud of having been a good businesslike official, thereby disposing, in his case at any rate, the time-honoured conception of the poet as an unpractical dreamer. He was certainly no mere dreamer at any period of his life; he appreciated beauty with extraordinary keenness, but, like a true poet, he was never contented with mere appreciation. He was determined to make his vision as clear to others as it was to himself.

"I saw Flecker once more, in December 1914. He was already visibly dying, and at times growing weakness numbed his faculties. But he was determined to do two things—to complete his poem, 'The Burial in England,' and to put his business affairs into the hands of a competent literary agent. The letters and memoranda on the latter subject which he dictated to me were admirably lucid, and I remember that, when I came to read them through afterwards, I found there was hardly a word which needed changing.

"One evening he went through the 'Burial' line byline with Mrs. Flecker and myself. He had always relied greatly on his wife's taste, and I may state with absolute certainty that the only two persons who ever really influenced him in literary matters were the Oxford friend I have already mentioned and the lady whose devotion prolonged his life, and whose acute feeling for literature helped to a great extent to confirm him in his lofty ideals of artistic perfection.

"Although he never really finished the longer version of the 'Burial' which he had projected, the alterations and additions he made that evening—'Toledo-wrought neither to break nor bend ' was one of the latter—were in the mam improvements and in no way suggested that his end was so near. To me, of course, that poem must always remain intolerably sad, but, as I re-read it the other day, I asked myself whether the casual reader would feel any trace of the 'mattrass grave' on which it was written. Candidly I do not think that even the sharpest of critics would have known, if he had not been told, that half the lines were written within a month of the author's death."

His letters, as is remarked above, were generally business-like and blunt. I have found a few to myself: they are almost all about his work, with here and there a short, exclamatory eulogy of some other writer. He observes, in December 1913, that a journal which had often published him had given "The Golden Journey" "an insolent ten-line review with a batch of nincompoops"; then alternately he is better and writing copiously, or very ill and not capable of a word. In one letter he talks of writing on Balkan Politics and Italy in Albania; in another of translating some war-poetry of Paul Deroulede's.

Another time he is even thinking of "having a bang at the Cambridge Local Examination... with a whack in it at B. Shaw." Then in November 1914 he says: "I have exhausted myself writing heroic great war-poems." He might comprehensibly have been in low spirits, dying there in a dismal and deserted "health resort " among the Swiss mountains, with a continent of war-zones cutting him off from all chance of seeing friends. But he always wrote cheerfully, even when desperately ill. The French recovery filled him with enthusiasm; he watched the Near Eastern tangle with the peculiar interest of one who 'knew the peoples involved; and in one delicate and capricious piece of prose, published in a weekly in October, he recalled his own experiences of warfare. He had had glimpses of the Turco-Italian War: Italian shells over Beyrout ("Unforgettable the thunder of the guns shaking the golden blue of sky and sea while not a breath stirred the palm-trees, not a cloud moved on the swanlike snows of Lebanon") and a "scrap" with the Druses, and the smoke and distant rumble of the battle of Lemnos, "the one effort of the Turks to secure the mastery of the Ægean." These were his exciting memories:

"To think that it was with cheerful anecdotes like these that I had hoped, a white-haired elder, to impress my grandchildren! Now there's not a peasant from Picardy to Tobolsk but will cap me with tales of real and frightful tragedy. What a race of deep-eyed and thoughtful men we shall have in Europe now that all those millions have been baptized in fire!"

Then in the first week of January 1915 he died. I cannot help remembering that I first heard the news over the telephone, and that the voice which spoke was Rupert Brooke's.

J. C. SQUIRE

James Elroy Flecker – A Short Biography

James Elroy Flecker was born on 5th November 1884, in Lewisham, London to father William Hermann Flecker, an Anglican clergyman and mother Sarah (née Ducat) both of Polish Jewish origin. Both had fled to England because of persecution when they converted to Christianity.

Flecker was baptized as Herman Elroy Flecker, but later chose to use "James". He was educated at Dean Close School, Cheltenham, where his father was the headmaster, and then Uppingham School before proceeding to Trinity College, Oxford, and Gonville and Caius College, Cambridge. While at Oxford he was greatly influenced by the last years of the Aesthetic movement there under John Addington Symonds, and became a close friend of the classicist and art historian John Beazley.

At this stage Flecker does not seem to have been greatly motivated by academic study. He only achieved third-class honours in Greats in 1906. This did not set him up for a job in either government service or the academic world.

After some frustrating forays at school teaching in 1907 he attempted to enter the Levant Consular Service, more properly known as "His Majesty's Consular service in the Ottoman dominions, Persia, Greece and Morocco". The job came with a salary of £200 per annum. However, if after two years the entrant failed the examinations his bond of £500 (mainly provided by his parents) would be lost. On the positive side the standard of entrants was generally rather low as the jobs outcome was not in the exotic European and world capitals but unattractive climates or dreary oriental provincial towns.

Preparations for the Student Interpreters' examination involved two years' study at Cambridge, learning the local languages. As we know academic study was not a motivator for Flecker and the first of these two years was at best far below what he could do. He was placed 4th out of 6 candidates, with the "clever but erratic" phrase marked on his file. Now knowing that all might now be lost Flecker realised that his primary ambition of a literary and poetic career was far from being certain and a back-up plan of a secure job had to be made safe. He duly knuckled down and passed the consular examinations with first-class honours. It was now reported to the Home Office that "Mr. Flecker has recovered the ground he lost last year in a really marvellous way and deserves the highest credit for the way he has worked during the last year".

He now entered the Levant Consular Service and in June 1910 was dispatched to the Ottoman capital of Constantinople, where he was attached to the British consulate.

However, Flecker's poetry career had made progress and he was beginning to garner praise for his poetry volumes including "The Bridge of Fire" from 1907 and "The Last Generation", a short novel in

1908. Works would now follow on a regular basis. He worked slowly but with great precision and paid far more attention to his writing than his job. Unfortunately, the then dreaded tuberculosis was also making progress in him. The preliminary symptoms were already apparent, and bouts of ill health were to alternate with periods of physical well-being woven with mental euphoria and creativity. He had already spent a period in back in England in the Cotswolds convalescing at a sanitorium. These episodes would now be a feature of his life.

On the boat to Constantinople, he fell in love with a Greek woman from Athens, Hellt Skiaderessi, and married her, in the face of parental anxiety about his lowly salary and his future health prospects, in May 1911.

He seems to have performed his consular duties, when he was well, in Constantinople, Smyrna and then, after September 1911, as Vice-Consul in Beirut, in a careless and rather sloppy manner. He and Hellt were always stretched financially and required frequent subsidies from home.

His continuing examinations in Ottoman Law were not properly prepared for. Some were failed and once he was very nearly dismissed, putting the £500 bond once more in danger of being forfeited. For unknown reasons the Foreign Office in London were tolerant over this putting it down to his ongoing battle with tuberculosis and tolerant of his extended periods of leave.

Flecker began work on "Hassan" during a stay on Corfu in the summer of 1911 where he was working on his Turkish for a forthcoming consular examination and was reading various works in Turkish, including a volume of farcical tales, in one of which a simple old man, Hassan, is duped over a supposed love philtre by a Jewish magician, Zachariah. Flecker set his rendition in Baghdad rather than Turkey and began work.

Hassan too was much revised, and the final version, which was to form the basis for the acting text—Flecker was adamant that it should appear on the London stage—was not made till Autumn 1914 when he was at Davos. During its three-year gestation it went from a play with pantomime elements to a drama of human disillusionment and a climax of high tragedy. (Sadly, with the brutal intervention of World War I and the need for elaborate and expensive staging it would not debut on a London Stage until 20th September 1923, although it had premiered three months earlier in a German translation in Darmstadt.)

A visit to Damascus for Christmas 1911, a city he was always enchanted by, provided inspiration for "The Gates of Damascus", a poem it is said "marks the high point of Flecker's achievement in the oriental mood, since it combines powerful and concentrated ideas with an assured and free manipulation of the Persian-style internal and external rhymes". Flecker would also describe this as his greatest poem. In 1913 he had written a friend saying "I consider this to be my greatest poem ... It was inspired by Damascus itself by the way. I loathe the East and the Easterns, and spent all my time there dreaming of Oxford. Yet it seems, even to hardened Orientalists, that I understand".

Much of Flecker's work was based on Islamic themes and is immensely satisfying. However, Flecker himself seems to be at growing odds with them in reality often demonstrating an increasing lack of sympathy and respect to them.

As Flecker's health continued to deteriorate he now spent the last twenty months of his life in sanitoriums in Leysin and Davos. Here he carefully revised and improved all his work, usually producing more disciplined and pleasing versions of his works.

James Elroy Flecker died on 3rd January 1915, of tuberculosis, in Davos, Switzerland. His death at the age of thirty was described at the time as "unquestionably the greatest premature loss that English literature has suffered since the death of Keats".

James Elroy Flecker – A Concise Bibliography

Poetry
The Bridge of Fire (1907)
Thirty-Six Poems (1910)
Forty-Two Poems (1911)
The Golden Journey to Samarkand (1913)
The Old Ships (1915)
The Collected Poems (1916)

Novels
The Last Generation: A Story of the Future (1908)
The King of Alsander (1914)

Drama
Hassan: The Story of Hassan of Baghdad & How he Came to Make the Golden Journey to Samarkand (1922)
Incidental music to the play was written by Frederick Delius in 1920, before the play's publication, and first performed in September 1923.
Don Juan (1925)

Other
The Grecians (1910)
The Scholars' Italian Book (1911)
Collected Prose (1920)
The Letters of J.E. Flecker to Frank Savery (1926)
Some Letters from Abroad of James Elroy Flecker (1930)